Helene J. Storm is a writer and poet. Her poetry reaches from an Emily Dickinson-like free poetry style to common verses in a traditional form. The "Desire to push the world in a certain direction", as George Orwell called it, and that many artists are moved by, is also a vital part of her writing. Especially with those topics she is most passionate about, such as women's rights, equality and freedom of speech.

In retrospect, this book is as much my family's book as it is mine; or more so. Without the tireless support and the most-likely often slightly exaggerated praise, I never would have finished this book, or started writing it for that matter. So, this is on you.

Helene J. Storm

I'll Draw an Iris on My Heart and Send It to You

AUSTIN MACAULEY PUBLISHERS™
LONDON • CAMBRIDGE • NEW YORK • SHARJAH

Copyright © Helene J. Storm 2023

The right of Helene J. Storm to be identified as author of this work has been asserted by the author in accordance with sections 77 and 78 of the Copyright, Designs and Patents Act 1988.

All rights reserved. No part of this publication may be reproduced, stored in a retrieval system, or transmitted in any form or by any means, electronic, mechanical, photocopying, recording, or otherwise, without the prior permission of the publishers.

Any person who commits any unauthorised act in relation to this publication may be liable to criminal prosecution and civil claims for damages.

A CIP catalogue record for this title is available from the British Library.

ISBN 9781398488311 (Paperback)
ISBN 9781398488328 (Hardback)
ISBN 9781035802395 (ePub e-book)

www.austinmacauley.com

First Published 2023
Austin Macauley Publishers Ltd®
1 Canada Square
Canary Wharf
London
E14 5AA

A quick expression of gratitude to the Austin Macauley Publishers, for the remarkable opportunity to have my poetry published and read. It is a dream come true.

Table of Contents

Political Poetry and Controversial Verses   **11**
- Mad King   13
- Might   14
- For Your safety   15
- White Dresses   17
- Black Doors   18
- Independence (Exit)   19
- I know   20
- Perfect   21

Emotional Lyrics and Life- Lesson Literature   **23**
- Unconquerable Soul   25
- Thunder   26
- 0   27
- XIII   28
- Catching the Wind   29
- Angels   30
- Eternity   31
- Hearts   32

Darkness	33
After All	34
Artists	35
Deep End	36
Remember	37
Magic I	38
Magic II	39
Victorian Flirt	40
Sticky Note	41
Yours	42
Guy	43
Song	**45**
Sophie, Sing With Me	47
Heroine's Journey	48
Lover	50

Political Poetry and Controversial Verses

Mad King

"Death," he called, "to those, who love me."
"Death," he called, "to those, who don't."
"Death to each and every one, who does not pray to me."

There's nothing so excruciating, nothing so bizarre,
As yielding power, standing tall, for those who really are.
It will start just small with corruption, manipulation and maybe,
Just a little murder.

But then the paranoia starts, as soon as they believe,
The very propaganda that they once used to feed.
He'll start to poison enemies, right after they were friends.
And still will think "I had no fault; it was merely defence."

So, he will keep on poisoning, believing they are threats, 'till each and every one is dead.
So, rule up on your throne.
There's no one left for you to rule,
So, rule until you're gone.

Might

For people who yield power, there are many mights,
The might to build a tower, I might protect my folk.
There might be a way to help you, through my power and my might.
And I might lead this land to hell, as long as it's on fire
For if people live in huts or cells, might is my lone desire.

For Your safety

One beat.
One drum.
Keeps going on.
Grows fast and faster,
Won't slow down.
I know they'll come.
But when?

All I seem to see is fear and all I seem to hear:

One beat.
One drum.
My heart beats fast.
It can't slow down.
The silence is deafeningly loud.
I hear them come.
But why?

I stopped saying what I thought
I only think that what I ought.

The drum.
There's nowhere now for me to run.
They're here.
Now it's swallowed me, my fear.
I drown.
Too loud.

That's what my teaching was about.
Don't talk.
Don't think.
If you want to stay undead.
Just quiet.
And still.
Leave in your mouth your tone!
Leave in your pen the ink!

White Dresses

White dresses on the street, marching for freedom of speech,
White flowers in their hands, to show that without force, they'll stand,
But as the ignorance of boots will trample on their petals cruelly,
A man of power will not care, if they wore a dress in white.
Only later, when they stop blooming, they might know the petal's spite.
For skirts that tore and grass that dried, they know whose fault it is, they died.

Black Doors

She was given feet to walk
And she has a mouth to speak
She was given eyes to see
And on the top of all
The head covered in silky hair,
A struggle to handle, a burden to bear.

For the hand that was given to *him*
Held trembling with anger a pistol within.
And the mouth that he received,
Screamed her further and further under his feet.

And when he used his blessings
And turned them to a curse,
Her feet were chained,
Her eyes, they burned

And nailed onto the blood-stained door,
With bundles of hair, was her torn-apart shawl.

Independence (Exit)

Independence is what we want,
In this co-dependent world.
And independence is what we'll gain
To get our country in a turn.

One day later, when it's done,
Maybe we'll understand,
It's not the shackles that we lost,
It was the helping hand.

So, on this day, maybe we'll see
Friendship was what it meant to be
We bit the hand that used to feed,
We kicked the union of which we dreamed.

I know

You could have resisted,
Said 'no', when he kissed you.
It's your choice what to do,
So, the blame of this it's all on you.

How dare you say no?
How dare you resist?
Is it not me, who knows when you want to be kissed?
I love you too deeply, for you to realise,
And I want you to much for you to despise.

My feelings are real, so yours must be too,
Therefore, it's no matter if you say no.
I must have you, in full and whenever I want
And you have no say, don't misunderstand.

Perfect

Lonely are those, striving for greatness.
Deathly the paths to immortality.
To beseech, to take a place among the gods,
One must leave behind… humanity.

So, before you climb to unmeasurable heights, Remember, you are alone in the skies.

Emotional Lyrics and Life-Lesson Literature

Unconquerable Soul

(A fusion of Henley, Angelou, Wordsworth, Ehrmann, Cooke and Guest for my father)

You are a child of the universe
No less than the trees and the stars.
Find comfort in yourself, find comfort in your cause
In the confidence of heaven's applause:
This is the Happy Warrior, this is he,
Who everyone living wishes to be.

Know, the harder you're thrown,
The harder you bounce.
Success is but failure turned inside out.
You'll rise, you'll rise in the story you own.

Don't quit, don't give up, though the pace seems slow,
You may succeed with another blow.
I know I shall find you unafraid,
For yours is an unconquerable soul.
You are the master of your fate,
You are the captain of your role.

Thunder

First light then sound.
That's how it goes.
First comes the sparkle in her eyes,
Then with the laugh, dimples on both sides
Of her peachy, pink, wide smile.

The thunderstorm, quite wrongly feared,
Now is my favourite time of years,
The only picture that I have,
That is worthy of the name.
No equal of her smile could be fitted in a frame.

So, bring me thunder, bring me light,
All the drizzle you can find,
To give me comfort, make me smile on so many lonely nights.

0

I do not ask for wealth or money
Or for power and my gain.
But do send, for I am lonely,
Just one snowflake down my way.

XIII

Do you know bad omens?
I do.
I met her just outside of town.

Her truths lead me to believe in death,
Her lips lead me to believe in sin,
And her foresight tattooed my everlasting frown.

Catching the Wind

I was catching the wind this morning,
But I think it got lost in my hair.
For the longer that I entangled,
The more it got lost up in there.

This evening, I tried tugging,
But I think the wind got attached.
For the harder I pulled,
The harder it scratched
My scalp as it clung to my hair.

Maybe they are wrong about wind being breezy,
Maybe it just wants someone to care.

Angels

Like three droplets in a web, three pearls caught on a string,
Side by side, light with light, on celestial a wing.
The stars reach out a hand to me, to raise me up, to sing,
Of hands like theirs right next to mine,
To holding those with broken spines.
Stand tall and proud, forget the hours spent,
With crooked heart, unheard, unseen, helpless and so bent.

Eternity

I'll meet you in the stars one day,
High above the clouds.
The realm of butterflies and birds,
Where angels make their rounds.

I'll hold you tight, I'll kiss your lips,
That moment I will see,
That nothing gets better than this,
Just me and you, and you and me,
In eternity.

Hearts

There are two kinds of hearts.
Those, whose broken hearts are wounds
That scar with every love that's lost.
And those, whose hearts get sore and strained,
And grow through pain, like muscles trained.

I could see from afar
That yours was a heart that would scar.
You keep breaking every time that you love
And the deeper you love, the deeper a dagger digs into your heart.

Darkness

Is it true, have you doubted my love last night,
But does not every moth get drawn to the light?
Does darkness not hunger to swallow the sun?
And do demons not prey on innocent ones?
How doubt you the depth of my devotion,
When you are the sky and I your pollution?
Your poison to the medicine.
I know you need better, but can't leave your side,
For I, I am darkness, and you are my light.

After All

Do you remember, when we last danced?
It was May, under roses of a white pavilion.
You were dancing in a circle, and I danced out the door.
I thought I was happy, and I thought it made you,
Past-me you were silly; how little you knew.
That conditional is only a two-letter word
And being in love works for others. And third,
Your mirror tells lies that only you heard.
You may not believe it, but what he said was true,
His love was sincere, and he wished so were you.

Artists

The true difference between artists and optimists is that optimists seek God, while artists seek immortality.

Deep End

I saw the deep end and jumped in head first.

Remember

We are living the memories of our future selves. We just don't understand yet, why this moment is so memorable.

Magic I

Magic is a rare delight,
Occurring only at the crack of dawn.
Or in the middle of the night.
Feeding you insanity, while nourished by the moon,
Only overcoming you in sleep, or when you're occupied.

Magic II

Magicians are a lie, or a trick of light,
For no one has the power, to control a magic's might.
To summon it, when wanted,
To reach out to it at night,
Is just once and only granted,
For the moon's delight.

Victorian Flirt

Death, hast thou called on me already?
Heaven, do I walk thy holy ground?
For I look upon an angel.

Sticky Note

And on the mirror was a sticky note that reminded me that I loved you.

Yours

But now that I have tasted the sweet bitterness of losing my heart, I never want to own it again.

Guy

I called myself 'guy'. It saves a lot of trouble, don't you think?
I have nothing to live up to, not a label to live by.
I was just 'guy'.
Sometimes it would be nice, of course, to have some kind of definition,
But this way, at least, I have room.

It was different for a friend of mine.
Her name was Joy.
Joy didn't make it long.
But who would with that name?

Song

Sophie, Sing With Me

Sophie once thought that she could be anything
That she could travel the world and earn her own living.
Sophie thought that she could be great at what she does.
She had to learn it's men who win, poor women's loss.

Sophie, sing with me,
About all the things we wanted to be,
About all our dreams that died before they lived.
Sophie, sing about all that you had to give.
Sophie, please, sing with me.

Sophie told me once she was afraid to go outside.
She said that she's just paranoid, so I told her 'yes' and lied.
I thought that I was saving her soul,
But I just made them break it twice, after making it whole.

Sophie, cry with me,
About all the times we thought we were free,
About every time they extinguished our flame.
Sophie, cry, it's not a women's game.
Sophie, please, cry with me.

Heroine's Journey

She ruffs up her skirt,
Wades alone through the dirt,
With her bundle and guilt on her back.
Walks her boots to her bone,
Carries problems alone,
Just to find, what it is that she lacks.

To realise it is just herself,
Her feelings propped up on a shelf,
Wanting to get dusted and claimed.
She's been losing herself all in vain.

Come back to you. Tell me the truth,
How do you dream to be?
There's no need to change,
For you to be brave,
If sword or if ball-gown,
The choice is yours.

She straightens her belt,
While twirling her veil.
She dances in circles without a soul.

Her blonde curly locks,
Fall over her tux,
As she smiles, 'cause she knows she is finally whole.
She can choose what she wishes to be,
And she gives not one fuck for conformity.
Red lips and black eyes can perfectly match,
As long as you don't listen to people's chit-chat.

I'll come back to me
I'll start to believe,
I can be whoever I wish to be.
I'll learn to be brave,
And for me not to change,
Just because of what people expect from me.

Let them talk
Let them worry.
This is a heroine's journey!

Lover

What do you cry for, lover?
Why do you cry?
Because the stars, like no other,
Can't meet in the skies?

What do you cry for, lover?
Why do you cry?
The stars move towards each other,
And they'll meet, when we die!

CPSIA information can be obtained
at www.ICGtesting.com
Printed in the USA
LVHW041141090223
739019LV00017B/1737